Following Jesus
Into the Blessing

Jerry Daley

with Jerome Daley

Jerry Daley
219 Mossy Spring Lane
Boone NC 28607

www.jerrydaley.com

© 2017 by Jerry Daley

Cover design: Jerome Daley

Images: Josh Daley

Interior layout: Jerome Daley

ISBN-13: 978-1974581306

ISBN-10: 1974581306

Rev. 08.29.17

CONTENTS

Introduction

Wrap-up

INTRODUCTION

Everyone wants to be blessed. Why wouldn't we? Although we may not use the word itself, most of us want a blessed life in the sense that we want life to work. We want to be happy. We want our work to succeed and our relationships to satisfy. There's nothing wrong with that; in fact, there's something very much right about it. We're just not quite sure how to pull it off.

In fact I'd be so bold as to say that humans make all their decisions thinking they will bring good into their lives. Whether they have the foresight to foresee the consequences…or get seduced by the emotion of the moment is the question. Essentially, we make hundreds of choices every day that we think will bring happiness (blessing) closer.

But we often choose poorly, don't we.

Proverbs 16:25 reminds us that our "compass" is broken. We make choices that seem right…but wind up bringing death into our souls instead. It's all quite frustrating. We want to be successful and satisfied, but we don't associate this with being blessed. So we wind up walking blindly past the very things God has engineered for our well-being. We unintentionally pick up curses instead.

When it comes to navigating our way in life, we might consider the Bible as the book that explains blessings and curses. The word "blessing" or "blessed" occurs 466 times, so we can be sure that God will help us align our attitudes, values, and behaviors toward those that fit who He is. These are the very qualities, as we'll find out shortly, that He delights to bless. And those things that do not align with His nature automatically lead us into the curse department.

The Beatitudes

Jesus' most basic message is summarized in the Sermon on the Mount in Matthew 5-7 and begins with an outline of eight attitudes and actions that he calls "blessed." We now call them the Beatitudes. These famous declarations immediately tell us that God's ways are unlike anything we've ever known or thought before. A completely different reality. Unique, startling, shocking…and often even unbelievable. Yet these eight truths comprise the secret to making life work. And isn't that what we most want?

Very early in his ministry Jesus began to unpack these eight principles, confronting every culture on the planet. I can only imagine the impact upon the first disciples. The word "stunned" comes to mind. In today's world I can hear it like this: *You've got to be kidding. Yeah right, but we live in the real world.*

The "real world" is a dangerous place, and we all carry the scars. But Jesus came and opened a secret door that makes the world safe again. He is the door (John 10:7), and following Him leads us into the life of abundance for which we're made.

I look back at how God has been teaching me these simple, transformative truths for fifty-one years, and I'm grateful for His patience and gentleness with me. Many times I have tried it first my way only to find that He is, of course, right. These eight principles, eight values, eight choices bring the blessings we yearn for, so let's explore them together.

This may be a good moment to do a quick soul-check. Where am I right now as it relates to God's path? Am I poor in spirit? When I'm hurting, do I go to God for comfort? Am I teachable, easy to lead? Am I hungering for my character to be like His? Do I care enough to pay attention to the feelings of others? As I search my heart, are my motives pure? Am I playing the role of peacemaker in my relationships? When I get hurt trying to do what is right, am I rejoicing?

Tough questions…and some you can probably relate to better than others. What Jesus is trying to do here is offer us a GPS for the soul. A map that leads to blessing with key landmarks to let us know if we're on course.

Darkness and Light

The map we've been using hasn't worked out too well. Matthew illuminates the pain of this world when he describes the world as "sitting in darkness…in the land and shadow of death" (Matthew 4:16). Yes, we know the darkness of life all too well, and our hearts yearn for something better.

In view of that yearning, Matthew's next words fall like a cool spring rain: "Upon them a Light has dawned." Finally, Jesus has appeared to illuminate our path! When we see Jesus, we see something radically different. We see Light…and something in us responds to the Light.

I occasionally meet idealists who admire the Beatitudes and speak of the beauty of living this way, yet attempt to walk the path without the Mapmaker Himself. Yes, these principles describe the best of human ethics, but they presuppose the necessity of walking with Jesus personally every step of the way. We can't navigate it on our own. God's invitation is to an intimate relationship where He guides us Himself, instructing and leading us in every moment. Ready to get started?

1. NEED
Uncovering What's Wrong

Blessed are the poor in spirit, for theirs is the kingdom of heaven (Matthew 5:3).

The way out of the darkness always starts in the same place: feeling poor in spirit. It's not that we don't know what this feels like, it's just that we usually hate the feeling. "Poor in spirit" feels, well, *poor*. Impoverished. Lacking. It's the opposite of the way I usually want to feel: powerful, capable, and confident. Jesus is basically saying that happiness comes when we feel like spiritual beggars. Yuck.

Those feelings are so alien to our innate desires that we spend a great deal of our lives trying to avoid exactly that feeling…and to fake it when we can't. And this is precisely where we tend to step off the path of blessing and make ourselves unhappy.

It's not unlike the toddler who gets into the "do it myself" stage. She wants to feed herself, dress herself, open the door herself, climb into the stroller herself. But for all her good intentions, she simply cannot. The capacity isn't there. So what *is* there in such neediness? Well, intimacy is there. The sharing of life, the partnership of a toddler with her parent is part of the unique preciousness of this stage of life.

So we can't go much further on the right path, the path of blessing, until we uncover what's wrong. Until we're willing to stop fumbling around with those shoelaces, frustrating ourselves, working our fingers bloody as it were, trying to be in control. The kingdom of heaven is closed to those in that condition.

If we were to trust Jesus at this point, we would not be afraid to embrace the unremitting sense of being needy. To acknowledge our inadequacy and need for God. To say, "Help, Daddy. I can't do it." No, we can't do it and that's okay. Daddy is here to do it, and this is the sole posture that allows us to walk the path of blessing. Until we get this right, we go no further.

Transparency and Vulnerability

Circle this: *When I feel poor in spirit, Jesus is giving me His help*. He opens the resources of heaven to those who feel their total need for God. This is also called *humility*, and it unlocks all the storehouses of God's generous supply. We need Jesus' assurance of being there for us in order to step into this kind of transparency and vulnerability. This is the place of surrender, and He gladly meets us at this point of our need.

Remember Jesus' story of the prodigal son? The one who squandered his inheritance in the middle eastern version of a Las Vegas strip only to be left penniless, friendless, and hopeless. It was when he came home without any hope in himself that he encountered, much to his amazement, the Father's arms, kisses, and tears. Being poor in spirit isn't a place we naturally like to go, but the more times we experience Jesus meeting us at this point, the more we learn to live into the light.

Jesus, the Son of God, was poor in spirit. Strange thought, isn't it? Jesus wasn't trying to prove Himself, to be self-sufficient, or to establish His own worth. And we're talking about God in the flesh! As the Son of Man, Jesus received all that He needed because He was poor in spirit. This is a profoundly different way to live, and this is our example to follow.

This posture was Jesus' starting point and the reality He lived in 24/7. This is what enabled Him to "do nothing of Himself, unless it is something He sees the Father doing." It was His path to "the Father abiding in Me does His works" (John 5:20; 14:10).

Most of us are hard-wired with a performance-based lifestyle. We instinctively try to measure up, be good enough, to prove ourselves. Have you figured out yet that this is the darkness? It's called pride, and this "old think" seems to live in our very bones and prompts us to resist transparency and to blame others for our failures.

When you get in that zone, you can feel the joy slipping away. Darkness hurts. So go to school on this feeling. Learn to spot your performance-based response and call it out! Identify that way of living as darkness and move in the opposite direction. Move toward humility and surrender.

You can't personally make yourself poor in spirit, but you can bring your neediness to Jesus and ask Him for His gift. He never turns down this request because this attitude lines up with His ways. Realigning our hearts to mirror His is Jesus' greatest desire.

The Pride of Competency

It's a funny thing about pride—it can show up as the feeling that "I'm supposed to be able to do this." This doesn't look like pride at first glance. It doesn't say overtly, "Hey, I'm good. I can do whatever it takes." We would recognize that! No, this is more subtle...but it's still pride. And it likes to sneak in and do its damage.

Discouragement and depression often follow the pride path. When we think we're supposed to be independently competent, and then realize we aren't, it makes us want to give up and shut down. Sometimes this is where God finds us, bringing the most gentle and kindhearted of rebukes. *Let go of your pride. Embrace humility. It's okay; this is how my kingdom works.*

Once we make the transition from *I'm no good; I can't handle this* to *I'm naturally weak so I have to rely on Christ*, then we have shifted into faith. And faith opens up God's realm.

My go-to verse is, "My grace is sufficient for you, for power is perfected in weakness" (2 Corinthians 12:9). I think Paul was shouting when he first heard this revolutionary truth. I live constantly in this truth; it's huge in my life. Power-through-weakness offers the most understandable, most approachable way into Jesus' words, "Blessed are the poor in spirit." Does that make sense?

The Kingdom of Heaven

I've been hinting at this already, but let's be clear: the path of humility opens up all the resources of God's kingdom. From this posture of neediness, we step right into all the richness and provision of God. Now that's a great trade.

Let's say that I'm feeling anxious about meeting with a new client—perhaps concerned I won't have the answers. So the "dark" version of me has to posture and inflate, using bravado to cloak insecurity. But the "light" version of me rests in Jesus, knowing that Christ-in-me is exactly what this client needs. So I'm confident, being who I am and bringing what I have, trusting the results to flow out of the storehouse of heaven.

Or you're exploring a new romantic relationship but feeling uneasy having been burned before. The pride of your competency illusion tempts you to either rush too fast to intimacy or to flee from intimacy and commitment. But God's power-in-weakness truth invites you to transparency and authenticity, moving at a wise, healthy pace.

If you've ever learned to water ski or snowboard, then you've already learned a powerful spiritual lesson: that when you "lean into the fall," you don't fall! Amazing, isn't it. And extremely counterintuitive. Because that movement runs against every natural instinct, we have to train ourselves and eventually develop new instincts. It's not unlike choosing poverty of spirit. Letting go of all our self-protections and trusting the One who holds us securely.

Let's summarize. Feeling poor in spirit is the most fundamental posture of the Christ-follower. The Christian life begins here and constantly returns here. When we're willing to let God hold our hearts in this vulnerable place, then God's provision opens to us.

What are the heavenly resources you need most right now? Can you trust God to provide exactly what you need without trying to conjure it up on your own? Can you feel the safety and security of bringing your emptiness to Jesus and leaning into that need? Then you are in good company…and ready to take the next step on the path to blessings.

Your Turn
Journal your reflections on this chapter.

- How easy do you find it to be transparent and vulnerable?

  _____

  _____

  _____

  _____

- Where do you most resist being needy?

  _____

_____

_____

_____

- When have you experienced the connection between feeling needy and being humble?

_____

_____

_____

_____

- What specific situation are you prepared to release in weakness and see what God will do?

_____

_____

_____

_____

2. COMFORT
Finding God's Arms

Blessed are those who mourn, for they shall be comforted (Matthew 5:4).

I'm sorry to say that I didn't "bother" God with this blessing for many years. I don't mean that I disagreed with it; I simply ignored it. I had no interest in mourning.

Jesus told a story about a man finding a treasure in a field and then buying the field in order to get the treasure. It implies that the man was actively looking for something, but he wasn't quite sure what. However, when he saw it, he recognized the treasure and used all the money he had to own it. Sometimes we have a hard time recognizing what is truly valuable until it suddenly becomes clear. That's what we're talking about here as we connect the dots between "blessing" and "mourning."

In real life few ever discover the "comfort" of mourning…and as a result, we are quick to discount what Jesus was teaching. No one ever comes right out and says as much, but if I could ask God, "How much traffic does this promise get?" I'm pretty sure His reply would be, "Not much!"

15

What experience could be more common to our humanity than mourning? Think about some of our words for this: pain, sorrow, disappointment, betrayal, failure, heartbreak. Or these: agony, anxiety, despair, grief, regret. We have many experiences with these emotions, but unlike Jesus we may not know the path to comfort. We may medicate when what we really want is comfort.

I can think of at least three reasons people do not experience God's healing comfort. Let's look at them.

1. We do not connect our pain with the Bible word "mourn." We *do* mourn but fail to make the connection. When that happens, the blessings God offers are left on the table untouched.

2. We assume that when we are hurting, the comfort should come automatically…but it doesn't work that way. Pain *qualifies* us for His comfort—but we have to *come* to Jesus in order to receive it!

3. A third reason we miss God's comfort is that we simply don't know how to be still long enough to receive it.

Getting Comfortable with Laptime

Go here with me. A man had two sons: Jack is nine and Rob is eight. Both boys had a terrible day at school. Each was chosen last during recess ball games. Both were punched and ridiculed by bullies as they walked home. By the time they got home, they were seriously dragging bottom.

Jack came in the house first, bloodied lip and tears still in his eyes, closely followed by Rob who stomped upstairs and slammed his bedroom door. In biblical language, they were both mourning, but watch what happens next.

Some might think that a nine-year-old is too old to climb into Dad's lap and let it all out, but that didn't stop Jack. He sobbed the whole story out into his father's chest, and Dad listened to every word, holding him tight and rocking him a little. No one could hear the words Dad whispered into Jack's ear, but in about 30 minutes Jack hopped down as a happy camper. *He had received comfort.*

But what about Rob? Silence. He kept everything held in, bottled up. Rob was hurting deeply with what we might call "unprocessed pain." He didn't come to Dad or share his grief with anyone. Instead he nursed it, rehearsing the painful slide show and wishing he could even the score. Mourning, yes. Comfort, no.

So Rob's not eight any more; he's thirty-eight. And he still has not learned to come and receive comfort, not from people and not from God. He has become a master at emotionally disconnecting from anything that hurts.

In the face of these many hidden traumas, Jesus came to lead us into His Father's "lap." Think about Jesus' many rejections, accusations, and insults. He became a pro at coming to Father for comfort, and He wants to lead us into this secret blessing. Father's lap can become your new favorite place as you learn to meet Him right in the middle of failures, disappointments, rejections, and injustices.

Processing Your Emotions

When was the last time you landed in the "mourning" category? Can you remember? When was the last time you felt *ashamed, disgusted, provoked, troubled, resigned, frustrated, neglected, disoriented, depressed, condemned,* or *jaded*? Why not place all your insecurities in the mourning category as well? Wow, that opens up some territory.

Not only might we fail to connect the dots between such emotions and God's invitation to comfort, we might not fully recognize these feelings when they show up, even when they are dominating our souls. We have a wide range of emotions, but we may not have learned to put name tags on them. I call these unprocessed emotions. Here are three questions I use in my journaling for just this purpose:

1. What seven or eight significant emotions have I experienced in the last 24 hours?

2. What do these emotions tell me?

3. What is God saying to me about them or through them?

This is a simple way to process your emotions with God.

Ah, but this still leaves the issue of whether or not I will come with my emotion in my hand to Father and sit with Him so that He can, indeed, love on me. He restores my soul…*if I come.*

Not too long ago, I felt like I was cheated out of a large sum of money. And for a while, it really ate at me: I felt taken advantage of, manipulated, disrespected. Those feelings generated the usual cocktail of anger and resentment. So what do you do with that?

Gradually, I sensed Jesus' invitation to come into Father's "lap" and pour out my frustrations. As I did, the anger began to dissipate, and I began to feel comforted. It's that simple—and that difficult. But the blessing came! I never cease to marvel that when God corrects me, I feel loved at the same time. Surprisingly, this is the essence of true happiness.

As I journaled about this exchange, I received another jolt of insight! Jesus was being a friend to me. Nan and I do this with one another, so I suddenly recognized that this was exactly what Jesus was doing with me: being my friend. I'd never seen this so clearly before.

Imagine having a friendship with the Son of God! It makes me want to be His friend back.

Your Turn
Journal your reflections on this chapter.

- Can you think of times when you've mourned but did not access God's comfort?

_____

_____

_____

_____

- How easy do you find it to come to Jesus when you are in need of comfort?

_____

_____

_____

_____

- In the story of the two sons, with which one do you identify most? If you see yourself in Rob, what would it take to step more into Jack's narrative?

_____

_____

_____

_____

- How do you experience God's correction as an invitation to friendship?

  _____

  _____

  _____

  _____

3. MEEKNESS
Yielding to God's Leadership

Blessed are the meek, for they shall inherit the earth (Matthew 5:5, ESV).

When I was a teenager, my parents gave me a present that many teens only dream of—my very own horse. They hoped this would keep me out of trouble…which was not entirely successful. As it turned out, my relationship with "Thunder" was a turbulent one.

I soon discovered that this mare had a mind of her own—and was not interested in taking directions from me! I would pull on the reins with all my strength, but that horse's mouth was as tough as nails. I eventually learned to lean as far over her neck as possible, grab the reins right beside her mouth, and saw away until she got the message.

Once she got to a gallop, she was unstoppable. Despite my best efforts to rein her in, I would have to jump off to escape more serious injury. She was not what we could call "meek."

Becoming "Meeked"

Interestingly enough, the word meekness used by Jesus is actually a military term referring to the taming of wild stallions that were then trained to be unafraid of thunderous noise or burning fire. A meeked horse can be ridden right into the heart of battle. It takes only a nudge, a single word, even the slightest shifting of the master's weight to bring it to stop, back up, or move sideways. I like to think of Jesus riding us into battle with such oneness of spirit.

To be "meeked" as a Christ-follower is to be easy to lead, easy to teach, easy to correct. I don't think Thunder ever got the message. She was a stubborn one, so we never experienced that kind of partnership together.

King David had some horse experience of his own and wrote in Psalm 32:9, "Do not be as the horse or as the mule which have no understanding, whose trappings include bit and bridle to hold them in check, otherwise they will not come near to you." And David foreshadowed Jesus' later words, "The meek shall inherit the earth" (Psalm 37:11 KJV).

We all start out in life pretty much like my mare, ornery and willful, reluctant to place ourselves under the dominion of another. But Jesus is the ultimate "horse whisperer," wooing us with His constant love and kindness until we begin to value what He values.

We are simply unaccustomed to thinking of meekness as a virtue, much less associating it with spiritual power. Yet Jesus uses this word to describe Himself (Matthew 11:29), which should give us a clue to why this character quality would bring blessing in our lives.

The Results of Meekness

So what kind of blessing would meekness bring us?

Let's ask some of God's "heroes." Numbers 12:3 tells us that "The man Moses was very meek, above all the men which were upon the face of the earth" (KJV). And where did Moses land? Rather than being weak, indecisive, or co-dependent, Moses becomes a bold, confident leader who inspires an entire nation and works spectacular miracles. Not bad.

Of course Moses doesn't start this way. As a young man, he was hard-headed and willful…what we might call today an "independent thinker." However we phrase it, it took a long time and some hard knocks to prepare Moses for his destiny as a meek leader. Just like it often takes for us. Thankfully, we serve a loving, patient God.

Just think about how tough it was to prepare another one of God's heroes, the apostle Paul! God had to throw him off his horse (I know a little of what that feels like) and blind him with supernatural light in order to break through Paul's willfulness and begin to sow a seed of meekness into that crusty soul. Jesus confronts him in his subdued state with another animal metaphor: "It is hard for you to kick against the goads" (Acts 26:14).

Farmers of the time would use a goad—a long staff with a pointed end—to nudge an animal, typically an ox, along the right path. But a willful animal would kick back against the goad, actually causing injury and pain for itself in the process. Moses and Paul were two who knew that experience well. And if we're honest, so do we.

It's only when we truly come to trust the direction and pace of our Master that we can relax and come into alignment with the Father's good intentions for us. At that moment in time we experience the blessing of yieldedness. Of sweet surrender. The blessing of meekness.

Jesus promised that the meek would inherit the earth...but what does that actually mean? I understand it to mean that, as we embrace this humble surrender, our destinies on the earth reveal themselves. The easier we are to be led, the more God is able to place us where we belong—in the relationships, vocation, and location of God's choosing for God's good purposes and our delight. That was Moses' and Paul's experience, and I observe it continually in the leaders I coach.

God is constantly inviting his frenetic, multi-tasking children off the treadmill of frantic activity and into a yoke He promises is easy and light. It is a submission, but it is the path that provides "rest for your souls" (Matthew 11:29-30). And that sounds like blessing to me.

Learning to love the privilege of submission is one of life's choice moments. *He loves me. I am safe. I can surrender my agenda for His.*

The blessings of Matthew 5 actually have a purposeful order: We experience our powerlessness in life circumstances, and that draws us toward being poor in spirit. Then our hurts teach us to climb into Father's lap and receive comfort. As this begins to take effect, we become less hard-headed, easier to lead. Meek. Which begins to create in us a fierce appetite for the ways of God. Let's go there next.

Your Turn

Journal your reflections on this chapter.

- What has been your past understanding of or experience with meekness?

  _____

  _____

  _____

  _____

- How would you now define meekness?

  _____

  _____

  _____

  _____

- How do you experience God taming ("meeking") the wild horse in you?

  _____

  _____

  _____

  _____

- What's your take-away from the stories of Moses and Paul?

  _____

  _____

  _____

  _____

4. PASSION
Wanting What Truly Satisfies

Blessed are those who hunger and thirst for righteousness, for they shall be satisfied (Matthew 5:6).

It was a question that changed my life on a Sunday morning as Nan and I sat in a traditional church in Big Spring, Texas. I had recently graduated from the Air Force Academy and was up to my ears in pilot training. The pastor was ambling along when out of his mouth came this jarring intrusion into my very being: "If you get where you're going, where will you be?"

His question rocked my world. I had worked hard to get through the Naval Academy Prep School and four years of the Air Force Academy. I was finally a Second Lieutenant, married, and pressing hard into my career. No one, I mean not a single person, had ever asked me such a profound question.

In my mind I quickly promoted myself to Brigadier General and asked myself, "So how does that feel?" My answer: *Not much different from being a Lieutenant except a bit more money and prestige.* At that moment I realized I was not going to have a military career. It would never satisfy.

So what about you? Would you like to engage this dangerous question? *If you get where you are going, where will you be?* It's another way of asking, *What matters most to you? What are you most passionate about?*

In our world, we are constantly told what matters most. Money, position, respect, power, pleasure, beauty, popularity, achievement, influence—the pursuit of these is modeled for us constantly by our society. By the people we know, by those we watch on TV. Houses, cars, fitness, degrees. Yes, we feel the internal pull; there is an attraction…and without something more compelling, we will default to such small passions.

Paul describes this dynamic in Romans 1:22-23, "Professing to be wise, they became fools, and exchanged the glory of the incorruptible God for an image in the form of [things] corruptible." Those passions—money, position, respect, etc—are not evil…*but they are easily corruptible*. Inevitably corruptible, we might even say, without a heavenly realignment!

Made for Glory

Truth is, God is the one most highly motivated for our good. We are hard-wired for glory; it runs deep in the architectural engineering of our souls by none other than the Creator Himself.

And it is the passion of fiery desire that is designed to fuel this journey toward glory. That glory comes from the image of God in which we are fashioned: "Let Us make man in Our image, according to Our likeness," God declares in the triune council in Genesis 1:26…and then blesses the results with the benediction of "very good."

Such goodness—or glory—is the desire of God for all His children. "For I consider that the sufferings of this present time are not worthy to be compared with the *glory* that is to be revealed in us" (Romans 8:18). Oh yes, we are made for glory. But when that glory is exchanged for such meager ambitions as physical beauty and human achievement, our destiny is thwarted.

We usually have to experience the emptiness and vanity of these small passions before God can awaken us to a glorious alternative…and we find that it is nothing less than God's very character that ushers us into the joy and satisfaction of heaven's blessings. Into the happiness of our eternal purpose.

Catching the Appeal of Righteousness

Righteousness is God's shorthand expression for this great glory of His good intent. What a surprise! How unexpected, that transformation towards God's character—what Galatians calls the fruit of the Spirit—would bring us such delight! "Love, joy, peace, patience, kindness, goodness, faithfulness, gentleness, self-control...[and] such things" is our first glimpse into the divine character to which we are invited (Galatians 5:22-23).

Happy and blessed are you, Jesus says, *when your heart burns with hunger and thirst for righteousness. I assure you that this passion will satisfy! Everything else comes up short; it tantalizes and deceives, but my character is like the most delicious meal. It delights and fulfills your every longing.* That's quite a promise.

What would it look like if we were to take Jesus seriously at this point? If righteousness in body, mind, and spirit were to become our all-consuming passion? We don't know what circumstances it will inspire, but we do have God's commitment that our hearts will be satisfied...and isn't that what we want most?

Finding Your Satisfaction

What do you want to be when you grow up? It's a question we were all asked when we were young. Later in life the question morphs to, "What's your major? What do you want to do?" It's sort of an adult version of the earlier question.

Our answers change over the years along with the questions. Maybe a *policeman* or a *dancer* becomes a *teacher* or a *pilot*. Maybe *missionary*, *engineer*, or *lawyer*. But think for a moment: Now we are not answering the childhood question at all. "Doing" has replaced "being." *What do you want to be?* is very different from *What do you want to do?*

If we are responding to Christ's invitation to "hunger and thirst," then our movement toward His character speaks to the priority of *being.* Your destiny has far more to do with who you are becoming as a person than your occupation. Did you catch that?

No doubt you have dreams, desires, hopes, and probably some goals along the journey…but if character is the main event, then we can begin to answer that childhood question, *What do you want to be when you grow up?* I want to be like Christ.

Listen to another version of the question. "What do you want Me to do for you?" Jesus asks blind Bartimaeus in Mark 10:51. *What is your great desire?* Jesus wants to know. *Why?* Because He wants to meet it! So how would you answer that question? Your answer will lead you down a road; righteousness will lead you toward your God-given destiny. Toward satisfaction.

So what does it mean when we *don't* feel satisfied with life? It may mean that we are looking in the wrong places. We are hungering and thirsting—but not tapping into the source that satisfies. Not connecting the dots between righteousness and our hearts' deepest longing.

The world doesn't accommodate "seniors" all that well, and I was complaining to God about this when He turned the light on: I was not satisfied because I was seeking something other than being like Him. Immediately I sank down into satisfaction: His gift.

Let's get practical. What does "hungering and thirsting" look like in our lives? When it comes to food and drink, we simply sit down to enjoy a meal. When it comes to feasting and drinking from God's righteousness, it looks like being with God: taking God's Word into our souls, holding God's purposes in our prayers, and fellowshipping with God's people around truths and activities that are righteous, that are redemptive in our communities.

Hunger and thirst speak to satisfying our appetites, so lean into what satisfies your appetite for God. A prayer walk in the woods, taking a meal to a shut-in neighbor, memorizing Scripture, reading spiritual books, serving in your local church—these are just a few of the practical ways you can engage God's righteousness and reap the blessing.

Looking at the Big Picture

Let's pause for a moment and pan out to the big picture. The diagram on the next page offers a graphic representation of these eight great steps in the spiritual journey. Take a look.

So far we have covered Beatitudes one through four. First, we feel our extreme need for God. Second, we learn to actually come to God in order to receive His comfort. Third, we become easy to lead in God's hands so He can take us into our destiny. Fourth, we begin to value God's ways so as to receive His character.

I have placed the Big Eight on a mountain to highlight the shift that comes here at principle number four. The first side of the mountain is where we are transformed personally—and Passion is the apex. Once we make the connection between God's character and our blessing, then life really starts to hum! God's passion becomes our passion, and our lives becomes an extension of His great love for planet earth.

The back side of the mountain is where we are empowered to transform others…and that's where we're going next.

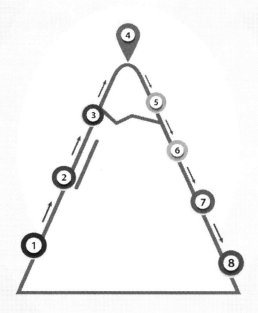

1. Need
- Feeling your neediness

2. Comfort
- Finding Father's arms

3. Meekness
- Becoming easy to lead

4. Passion
- Receiving His character

5. Compassion
- Receiving the ability to care

6. Purity
- Finding your true heart

7. Peacemaking
- Your mission on Earth

8. Joy
- Finding victory in suffering

Your Turn

Journal your reflections on the questions we have raised in this chapter.

- If you get where you're going, where will you be?

  _____

  _____

  _____

  _____

- What would it look like if righteousness were to become your most important goal in life?

  _____

  _____

  _____

  _____

- What do you want to be when you grow up?

  _____

_____

_____

_____

- How are you feeling drawn to respond to God's invitation to "hunger and thirst" for Him?

_____

_____

_____

_____

5. COMPASSION
Receiving the Ability to Care

Blessed are the merciful, for they shall receive mercy (Matthew 5:7).

I told a friend recently that I'm a recovering Type-A. What I mean by this is that compassion is not my natural default! I'm visionary, motivated, task-oriented, and determined…but I'm not naturally sensitive and caring. When that shows up inside me, I know that God is in the house!

When I see people on the streets or coming out of buildings, it's much more common for me to make instant judgments. No, compassion is not my first instinct. But over the years, my desire to be compassionate has grown considerably.

Don't you cherish the treasure of a friend who is willing to listen to your victories and heartaches…and care deeply? Someone who can go there with you and value what they hear—just because it comes out of your heart? This is precious beyond words.

Not everyone has either the sensitivity (by nature) or the maturity (by growth) that enables him or her to share life with you at this level. Yet it's something deep in the heart of God, our Father, as well as in our Savior-Friend Jesus. "Seeing the people, He felt compassion for them, because they were [stressed out] and [discouraged], like [uncared-for] sheep without a shepherd" (Matthew 9:36). What would it take for our hearts to be so moved?

Slings and Arrows

The pain in our world is off the charts, despite our affluence and comfort in the western world. Children with cancer, debt and bankruptcy, betrayal in the workplace, the divorce epidemic, Parkinson's and dementia, police shootings, abuse, neglect.... The list goes on and on.

When you move beyond the individual pain to the global outcry, the volume simply increases: genocide, starvation, pandemics, people-group displacement, suicide bombers, and city-leveling tsunamis...how can we even process such grief and loss? It threatens to undo us.

In spite of our human limitations, Jesus demonstrated what compassion looks like and speaks to the human capacity for compassion when filled with the divine. Consider the woman caught in adultery in John 8:1-11. The crowd was abuzz with blood thirst, almost riotous with violent malice. Some were focused on trapping Jesus. Others were focused on the woman, hardened by their religious fundamentalism. And probably some were simply curious bystanders.

But Jesus defused the mob with His calm authority and gentle spirit. His mercy did not condone bad behavior; instead it reached past behavior to the heart of this woman's worth and identity as a child of God. His justice was restorative, calling this woman out of her bondage and into freedom. Mercy is what liberates people from bad behavior!

How do we respond in situations where people are being criticized and judged? Do we get caught up in the mob's self-righteous condemnation, or do we reach for the hurting soul with love and care? Jesus shows us the way to the blessedness of compassion. He is utterly consistent in His reach for the "least of these."

From His gentle rebuke of the rich young ruler (Mark 10:17-22) to His weeping over the heartbreak of Lazarus' death (John 11:1-44) Jesus exemplified mercy. He was deeply touched by the sorrows and suffering of those who crowded around him for a healing touch or kind word.

We all want to be on the receiving end of such mercy, don't we! Jesus cares for us because He understands our condition. "For we do not have a high priest who is unable to empathize with our weaknesses, but we have one who has been tempted in every way, just as we are—yet he did not sin" (Hebrews 4:15 NIV).

Empathy and Action

Empathy is our modern word for the ability to place ourselves in other people's condition and experience some of what they are feeling. This is the precursor for extending mercy. First, to feel with another and second, to extend the hand. Empathy requires action.

Perhaps Jesus' best illustration of this connection is the story of the Good Samaritan—a man who had least cause to care about the plight of a mugged foreigner, beaten and helpless on the side of the road. Those who had most cause to care—the priest and the Levite (professional soul-tenders by trade) dodged the discomfort of both empathy and action. Perhaps they justified it in their minds by noting other worthy activities that would be delayed if they stopped to help.

This challenges me profoundly, knowing that I too encounter deep discomfort when confronted by the raw neediness of those who are hungry or homeless. God has to pry open our hearts and give us both courage and compassion to reach past that instinctive withdrawal, to empathize, and then to act in mercy. To the extent that we fail this test, we miss our true potential as children of God who live in solidarity with God's other children who hurt.

Or maybe the priest and the Levite weren't too busy; maybe they were just judgmental. "Shouldn't have been out on this road alone, no sir! He was just asking for trouble. What was he thinking!" Sometimes we actually blame those who have been most injured. Nothing shuts down mercy faster than blaming the wounded.

Whether it was busyness, discomfort with such raw neediness, or a judgmental spirit, it's fair to ask ourselves: *Were these two religious leaders happy? Were they blessed?* Not knowing anything else about them, we can pretty confidently deduce that they were not...because this is a universal law God has established. Being merciful brings a blessing!

Love: The Epitome of Mercy

The continuum of compassion – empathy – action culminates in the simplest and most challenging character quality of all: love.

There is no desire of our hearts that gets as quickly diverted—and no biblical command that gets as easily ignored as this one. But love is the prime directive. "Love is the fulfillment of the law," Paul tells us in Romans 13:10. In other words, to the extent that we live in love, we live in the fullness of God's character and heart for planet earth.

When asked to identify the greatest commandment from among the thousands of the Mosaic Law, Jesus famously sums it up as love. "Love the Lord your God with all your heart and with all your soul and with all your strength and with all your mind'; and 'Love your neighbor as yourself.'" (Mark 12:30-31).

In light of this we could rightly view the eight Beatitudes as a love explosion: a parsing of what love looks like in a variety of situations. And mercy is one powerful expression.

The Vulnerability of Receiving

Here's another thought. As difficult as it is to extend mercy, we sometimes even resist receiving it. It's not that we don't want mercy because at a heart level we certainly do. But we sometimes face two strong impediments to actively receiving it.

First, in order to receive we have to acknowledge our extreme neediness. We have to admit that we are the wounded traveler, bloody and unable to help ourselves...and this is an extreme vulnerability. To push the metaphor, sometimes it feels better to throw a cloak over our beaten body and pretend we're just sleeping on the roadside. This takes us right back to being "poor in spirit," doesn't it?

The other obstacle that confronts us at times is that we too carry the judgmental spirit of the priest and Levite. We not only judge others, we judge ourselves! Today we call this dynamic "shame," and it is the flip side of pride. We ought to have been more careful; we should have known; maybe we even deserve the suffering we are now experiencing...so don't be showing me any mercy!

To enter into the blessedness of the merciful, we have to surrender such lame excuses and own our neediness, our brokenness so that we can receive. If you can't receive it, you surely can't give it. God invites us into the security of being beloved children, and from this solid identity we can give and receive...and experience the happiness that comes with both.

Your Turn

Journal your reflections on this chapter.

- What is your ability to "go there" with people and feel what they are feeling, whether they are struggling or rejoicing?

_____

_____

_____

_____

- How easily do you empathize with the needy? What makes it difficult for you to feel merciful?

_____

_____

_____

_____

- Do you relate to either of the difficulties in receiving mercy…and how can you invite Jesus into that place?

_____

_____

_____

_____

- How might you grow in your ability to experience what Jesus is talking about in extending mercy to others?

_____

_____

_____

_____

6. PURITY

Finding Your True Heart

Blessed are the pure in heart, for they shall see God (Matthew 5:8).

What would it be like to have a pure heart? I'll bet you've never even heard this question posed before. I mean, come on! Whoever imagined humans in this condition? What group of people even longs for such a thing?

Purity is unfamiliar territory, but it is Jesus who demonstrated such a life and beckons us to follow Him into tasting some of Heaven now, even if it is intermittent.

As we follow Jesus, the Man, the Savior, we slowly begin to experience an awakening sense of need for what He describes as purity of heart. The desire itself is a metamorphosis. Every tiny "sip" of heart-change makes us long for more; it is simply freedom. And who would have guessed?

Paul lets us in on the secret in 1 Timothy 1:5, "But the goal of our instruction is love from a pure heart and a good conscience and a sincere faith." He tells us that the ultimate goal of all his teaching and instruction in the churches is love...*and that this love for others must be held in a container that is pure.* A "pure heart," a "good conscience," and a "sincere faith" comprise a pretty tight cluster! All of these point to the same core dynamic: a singleness of intent and engagement that is fully Godward.

Intent is where purity begins: the motivation of our hearts to be aligned with His. It's not just what we do, but—even more importantly—why. It is only as our motivations are refined that the purity journey begins.

This purity and sincerity are the opposite of the double-mindedness James describes as "the surf of the sea, driven and tossed by the wind" (1:6). Uncertain, uncommitted, conflicted, ambivalent—these are the symptoms conquered by purity of heart. Of course we don't start there…and it's doubtful we ever even end there in this lifetime, but without question this is the spiritual journey of ongoing transformation. Purity is the path toward the blessed life Christ calls us to occupy.

Part of the blessing that surrounds purity is that we do indeed find our true hearts. To the extent that our hearts are purified we find who we are meant to be, and we are empowered to live more and more in the benefits of God's world. Purity is its own reward. We cannot purify ourselves by ourselves, yet neither can we be purified outside of our active pursuit and participation, so let's talk about that next.

Ascending the Hill

King David presumably wrote Psalm 24 to be sung upon the occasion of transferring the Ark of the Covenant out of the home of Obed-Edom and up Mount Zion into the new Tabernacle he had constructed. "Who may ascend into the hill of the LORD? And who may stand in His holy place? He who has clean hands and a pure heart, who has not lifted up his soul to falsehood and has not sworn deceitfully. He shall receive a blessing from the LORD" (Psalm 24:3-5).

This was a time of soul-searching for David, and it now becomes a template for our own soul-searching. We know intuitively that to approach the presence of God requires something of us: it challenges and changes us. And if we're not willing to be changed, then the experiential presence of God is forfeit. Clean hands, a pure heart, a commitment to truth—these were the passport to blessing then, and so they are now.

As we've alluded to, this calls us to the daily transformations of confession, repentance, and obedience. In other words as we recognize places of impurity, we offer these places to God in the firm hope of His refining work within us. Then, of course, we have to walk out that inner change in ongoing obedience in the power of the Spirit.

Let's unpack that practically. *Confession* is our declaration to God that we recognize impurity within us. We name it for what it is and take responsibility for it. *Repentance* is our determination to change courses—to turn away from impurity and toward God's ways. *Obedience* is our demonstration of putting God's truth into action in our lives...by the grace that strengthens us.

So purity is instigated by God and empowered by God, yet we are active participants. Paul was a straight-shooter with his disciple Timothy: "Flee from youthful lusts and pursue righteousness, faith, love and peace, with those who call on the Lord from a pure heart" (2 Timothy 2:22). As we seek purity and flee from impurity, our hearts are transformed and we experience the blessings of God's ways...specifically righteousness, faith, love, and peace.

That sounds like a life worth pursuing!

A Clean Conscience

A little earlier we looked at the link between purity of heart and a clean conscience; let's go a little deeper there. As we respond to God's invitation toward purity, not only do we experience His blessings on our lives, there's a great byproduct: our consciences become ever more sensitive to the gentle leading of the Holy Spirit.

And this is a big deal.

While some of our turnings away from God are, if we're honest, intentional, others are done out of ignorance. Because the conscience is not sensitive. God has to re-train our hearts to become increasingly attuned to the Spirit's voice. This is very similar to becoming "meeked," as we explored in chapter three. This sensitivity is a priceless gift as it empowers us to keep drawing closer and closer to God in purity. Listen to these words...

"Since we have a great priest over the house of God, let us draw near with a sincere heart in full assurance of faith, having our hearts sprinkled clean from an evil conscience and our bodies washed with pure water. Let us hold fast the confession of our hope without wavering, for He who promised is faithful" (Hebrews 10:21-23).

This passage highlights both God's part and our part. The cleansing and purifying is all of God; however, the drawing near and holding fast are ours. This is the divine partnership we are called to walk in each day.

Face to Face

The promise to those who are pure in heart is mind-boggling: *we shall see God!* Purity allows us to behold Purity. Having our hearts cleansed washes away those very impediments that blind us from perceiving the beauty of God and delighting in the intimacy He offers.

Paul says, "But we all, with unveiled face, beholding as in a mirror the glory of the Lord, are being transformed into the same image from glory to glory, just as from the Lord, the Spirit" (2 Corinthians 3:18). This beholding begins now and increases with our purity "from glory to glory."

Grace draws us ever onwards…and eventually, the face-to-face will have no mediation, no impediment. "For now we see in a mirror dimly, but then face to face; now I know in part, but then I will know fully just as I also have been fully known" (1 Corinthians 13:12).

Does this thrill you as much as it does me? This promise is not merely for some spiritual elite, not just for professional ministers. No, all of the eight blessings to which Jesus calls us are for the taking. For all of God's children then and all of God's children now.

Here's another mindboggling thought: Psalm 25:14 implies that God has secrets that He is willing to share with those who seek Him. What are God's secrets? I think they are insights into who God really is and what He is doing in the world. It's what we might call friendship with God...and this kind of "seeing" God belongs to the pure in heart.

The intimacy of purity is where He is taking us! Many cleansings, many restorations, but oh the delicious joy of such freedom. Let's keep moving out of the darkness and into the light.

Your Turn
Journal your reflections on this chapter.

- How do you relate to King David's desire for "clean hands and a pure heart"? When have you struggled with wanting a pure heart?

_____

_____

_____

_____

- When have you done something that was fine in itself but done for the wrong reason? Can you recognize when God tests your motives in order to purify you?

_____

_____

_____

_____

- How accessible does purity of heart feel to you personally? Does your heart hunger to see God?

_____

_____

_____

_____

- What might God want to freshly cleanse in your conscience today? What is God showing you about your motives? Take that purifying step right now toward blessing.

7. PEACEMAKING
Stepping Into Your Mission

Blessed are the peacemakers, for they shall be called the sons of God (Matthew 5:9).

I was driving into town on an errand today when I suddenly realized that I was operating in my own full-blown soul strength. I was in high gear, and I was pushing. You know what that feels like, right? Face pinched in frustration, resisting obstacles, pushing. Internally willing all the people and circumstances in my life to get in line with my plan for the day. It wasn't working. In truth, it never does.

Without realizing it, I find that I instinctively try to control situations. People. And you know, things. Often, now that I'm a Christ-follower, I want something good to happen, but I can get my will wrapped around a good thing…and then it is no longer what God intended and it doesn't bring divine results. Instead of creating peace, it creates stress.

The good news is that our striving doesn't freak Jesus out…and needn't freak us out either. Freedom is one inner shift away. In the car I went immediately to David's standby, "I will bless the

Lord at all times" (Ps. 34:1) and invited Jesus into my uptightness. Then, like David, I spoke to my soul, *Slow down, soul. Slow down...* and in minutes I was back in the peace. What a relief! Losing our peace saps the joy out of life in a heartbeat. Recovering peace is like a cool drink of water.

Following Jesus into the blessing means that He is training us for His Peacemaker Team—and peace is an inside job. Long before we can be a source of peace to others, peace begins on the inside of us!

My little driving incident is a small but real example of Colossians 3:15, which calls us to "Let the peace of Christ rule (or *umpire*) your hearts, to which...you were called." There's nothing quite like it. The entire calling of our lives—as spouses, parents, workers, leaders—rests upon this bedrock of Peace ruling the roost of our hearts. Without peace we accomplish little that lasts.

There are, of course, much greater tests than my little "soul fit," but living in the peace of God in the little things is part of training for when greater pain is involved. Sometimes this internal peacekeeping is downright tough. The Peacemaking Team isn't for sissies.

Managing Your Internal Peace

What percentage of the time would you say that you live in a state of internal peace? If you're like me, that question challenges deeply.

God designed the human soul to function with an inner stability that is hard to come by in a fallen world. People seek it everywhere. In a sense we have no choice; it's in our DNA. We see it in how people self-medicate with all sorts of things, things that end up making life even harder. Peace is compelling but elusive...until we are touched by God.

As Christ-followers we know the foundational truth that *we have peace with God through our Lord Jesus Christ* (Rom. 5:1). Unfortunately we don't always stay there; we frequently get sucked back into the deception of trying to rule our world. Trying to be strong again.

Our daily battle for peace is a measuring rod for knowing how aligned we are, moment by moment, with God's rule.

Everyone's peace gets disturbed. Maturity can be measured by how quickly we recognize its absence and move back into it. This is the "let" part in Paul's admonition to "Let the peace of Christ rule"—this is your part in opting into Jesus' peace offer.

Another facet of this soul maturity is paying attention to what actions decrease or increase our sense of inner peace. He likes it when we stay close, and when we do, we like it too! So step one in becoming a Peacemaker is letting God's peace more consistently rule your soul.

Multiplying Peace

As we learn to keep ourselves in the peace of God, the presence of God more richly abides in us and emanates through us—and that gets exciting fast. Because the world is so lacking and desperate for peace, people are intuitively drawn to us when we are living in its freedom.

You've heard the old expression, "You can lead a horse to water, but you can't make it drink." If we turn that phrase around, we see that we can't force peace on those who are committed to their anxiety, but we can model the benefits, we can invite them into its sweetness, and we can hook hungry hearts up with the Prince of Peace.

How do we do that?

"A gentle answer turns away wrath," Proverbs tells us (15:1). This is a form of peacemaking. When we meet hostility with humility, a peaceful current flows through the room. What else?

Welcoming the stranger, feeding the hungry, visiting the imprisoned—these are all peacemaking activities that Jesus says are ultimately done unto Him as we practically do them for others (Matt. 25:34-40). Assisting an elderly man, encouraging a harried mom, calming an anxious employee…the applications are endless, but peace is the outcome when we engage Jesus' mission. This is step two: the multiplication of your peace.

Resolving Conflict

As instruments of God's peace we also have opportunities to, not only help settle the choppy waters of one person's soul, but also help bring reconciliation between two or more people in conflict with one another. This is a particular grace open to us all, and we are never more in alignment with the purposes of God than when we facilitate the healing of relational breaches around us. This is part of our answer to Jesus' prayer in John 17:11, "that they may be one even as We are."

Conflict arises when people have different agendas, values, or priorities that wind up at cross purposes with the agendas, values, and priorities of other people. Even when both agendas may be good. But feeling disregarded in our agendas, we instinctively armor up and move into defensive posture. And the result is varying degrees of conflict, from minor annoyances to full-blown feuds.

As peacemakers, we have the opportunity to listen, to care, to offer respectful affirmations, and to help people lower their shields so they can engage their "foes" with humility and kindness. To the degree we have influence, we can lead warring factions toward vulnerability, repentance, and godly confrontations. This is part of our mission, all of us. Step three.

It's worth mentioning that there is a huge difference between a superficial keeping of the peace—the effort to ignore or cover up conflict—with true peacemaking that resolves conflict and heals relationships. The former is a mask and mockery of the real thing—like sweeping the proverbial dirt under the rug. The dirt doesn't go away, and it may well induce rot and decay. God is after something much more expansive and life-giving.

Jesus says something else remarkable about the ministry of peacemaking—He says that we will be recognized as God's children. Because God is the chief Peacemaker! Peace is a heavenly commodity; the world is powerless to generate enduring peace.

This recognition as God's children is both a testimony to all those observing or experiencing the entry of peace into turmoil, and it is also an affirmation of the intimacy we carry with the Father. To the extent that we mirror and manifest God's heart for reconciliation, we draw near to God. As we manifest the love of God where it is needed most, we get the overflow. Blessings are multiplied all around, and that's the point.

Your Turn

Journal your reflections on this chapter.

- What is your experience with managing your inner peace? How important to you is living in His peace?

  _____

  _____

  _____

  _____

- How quickly do you recognize the absence of peace…and how quickly can you step back into it?

  _____

_____

_____

_____

- How are you learning to be an agent of peace, inspiring and equipping others toward healthy community? Is there someone with whom you need to make peace?

_____

_____

_____

_____

- Where are you showing up as God's representative, advocating for peace in the midst of others' conflict?

_____

_____

_____

_____

8. JOY
Finding Victory in Suffering

Blessed are those who have been persecuted for the sake of righteousness.... Blessed are you when people *insult you and persecute you, and falsely say all kinds of evil against you because of Me. Rejoice and be glad...* (Matthew 5:10-11).

This one is my vote for the least popular blessing of Jesus' series! Are you with me on this?

The fact that the only sinless man in history was publically crucified pretty well tells the story regarding our world. He was persecuted for the sake of righteousness every step of the way. His love for the Father and His purity of heart provoked every hidden evil. Can His followers expect less?

Jesus' invitation was and is, "Follow Me." So we know who we are following, yet it seems to always come as a surprise: not the blessing part but the *insult and accusation* part. We are slow to learn that suffering is part of the package in this world...and even slower to see that pain can be an avenue for blessing.

People who do not follow Jesus have their share of rejection and criticism too; it's part of living in a broken world. But they must be mystified indeed by Jesus' pronouncement of a blessing upon this aspect of life. You can almost hear them mumble, "You've got to be kidding!" But no, He is not kidding. All these unpleasant experiences Jesus is describing can actually lead us to joy. Let's dig down on that.

Jesus the Joyful

I think it's safe to say that Jesus was the happiest person to ever walk this earth. Despite a host of internal and external difficulties—childhood transience, the misunderstanding of His parents, the early death of his father Joseph, and then a whole litany of more aggressive challenges once He started ministry— Jesus carried a peaceful spirit and joyful presence wherever He went.

How do you reconcile those contradictions?

Luke's version of the Beatitudes speaks even more forcefully to this paradox: "*Be glad* in that day (the day you are hated, excluded, insulted, and rejected) and *leap for joy*, for behold, your reward is great in heaven" (6:23). *Who does that?* I'll tell you who—it's the person who sees his or her reward! Who actually experiences this sense of solidarity with Jesus and is enriched by His affirmation.

70

Christ Himself found a way to bring victory into His greatest personal sacrifice: "who for the joy set before Him endured the cross, despising the shame, and has sat down at the right hand of the throne of God" (Heb. 11:2).

We're talking about following Christ, right? Well, He leads us into this revelation and thus the experience of being blessed right in the very middle of the persecution. That is the epitome of living in God's kingdom—where God's reward becomes more real than our physical or emotional cost.

Because of Me

If you are an American as I am, our experience with persecution is pretty meager in comparison with those of other eras and geographies who have endured loss on vastly different scales. Yet even there, God's words remain true. Suffering for doing right, speaking right, and standing up for the right is a gateway to joyful victory.

It is the "because of Me" factor that grants us access to joy in the midst of pain. This is also what separates the general promise of blessing in Beatitude number two ("Blessed are those who mourn...") from the more specific blessing here of celebrating persecution because of our commitment to follow Jesus.

Even if we aren't being forced to renounce our faith in the face of torture, we still have legitimate points of suffering for Christ. You might lose a promotion for championing financial integrity in your workplace. You might be socially shunned in your school for resisting moral temptation. You might lose money or friends or desirable opportunities if you commit to the path of righteousness.

If you take a stand for truth "because of Me," you might well be insulted or slandered. Can you find the blessing in that?

Passing the Test

Receiving an evil response when you are acting to uphold the good—that is a serious character test. We don't pass all our tests the first time around, do we? But God is faithful to keep bringing us back to the important ones so that we can be transformed into His image. That is what honors Him…and that is what satisfies us. We are made to become these God-formed men and women who can be the hands and feet and mouthpiece of God in the world.

Paul highlights this very quality in Philippians 1 where he describes the test of his unjust imprisonment. This is definitely a "because of Me" situation, right? And in the midst of that hardship—a first century prison must have been a pretty rotten place—he describes how "my circumstances have turned out for the greater progress of the gospel.... and in this I rejoice" (1:12, 18). Paul was able to see his suffering from God's perspective and then reframe it as an authentic blessing.

What is beautiful is seeing those who have followed Jesus through the fire, who have passed their tests, then tap into the blessings that Jesus promised. Their joy is contagious. They are seasoned warriors. There is a quality about them that only comes by staying close to the Savior-Shepherd-Friend when the cost is high.

May we all radiate His joy when we find ourselves tested by pain. That is victory indeed.

Your Turn
Journal your reflections on this chapter.

- How do you relate to the idea of Jesus as the happiest man on earth?

_____

_____

_____

_____

- What experiences have you had with being wrongly treated because you were following Christ and doing what was right? How did you respond...and what did you learn from it?

_____

_____

_____

_____

- When have you experienced joy in the middle of walking through a difficult experience?

_____

_____

_____

_____

- If you had to rewrite this Beatitude in your own words, how would you describe its message?

_____

_____

_____

_____

WRAP-UP

At the very beginning of this book, we talked about how Jesus came to bring light into our darkness. How we often foolishly or ignorantly choose the darkness. Sometimes we even prefer it! But we are made for the Light.

Whoever has the influence to define what is blessed casts a big shadow. Jesus Himself claims this right, but that doesn't stop the forces that shape our culture from assuming very different paths to happiness and blessing.

Because our world doesn't typically score God's "Top Eight" very high, to follow Jesus is quite an adventure. You will never be bored. Challenged yes…and blessed in ways that make others want to be around you.

Jesus is the Light! Jesus shows us how to live. How to walk in the ways that satisfy and delight us. How to make relationships work. How to live at peace with God and other people. But in closing I want to point out something you may not have noticed yet: each blessing in this list builds upon the one before.

Yes, the Beatitudes are connected like a chain. Each blessing lays the groundwork for the next one. Let's take a look.

An Ascending Spiral

The first blessing is a counterintuitive call to being poor in spirit—feeling spiritually starved, hungry, needy. The humble embrace of this uncomfortable feeling opens us up to the realities of heaven and the ways of God. It's like a whole new world that thrills us, amazes us, and hooks us forever.

This opening of the "kingdom of heaven" re-wires our thinking so that we can find comfort when suffering comes (blessing #2). We don't automatically understand how to receive God's comfort, but poverty of spirit is a prerequisite for learning how to meet God in the midst of disappointment, betrayal, or injustice.

As the miracle of divine comfort manifests in our experience, we become candidates for meekness (blessing #3). The combination of spiritual neediness combined with spiritual comfort begins to break our stubborn wills and make us easier to lead.

See how this is working? We rarely jump immediately to finding joy in persecution. That's a 400-level class! We have to start with the basics before we're ready for the advanced stuff. These truths layer one upon another, like a high-quality plywood, and yield a composite strength that is remarkably powerful.

Once we begin to yield to the Master's guidance and take hold of the quality of meekness, Jesus is able to lead us to inherit what God always planned for us: His purpose, our destiny (blessing #4). And this is worth some clarification. Sometimes we carry dreams that are different that what Father has chosen for us, which will lead us to either chafe or trust.

Psalm 139 assures us that body and soul were woven together by God in the secret place…and that every day of our lives was hand-crafted for us by God. The intimate care and choices of God for our destiny come through powerfully in David's reflection. Psalm 37 extends that idea with the promise that those who delight themselves in the Lord have their desires shaped and met by a good Father. So we can follow Jesus into our God-given destiny with confidence and assurance. Make sense?

Now look at the connection between being poor in spirit and being hungry and thirsty for God. Our sense of emptiness drives the spiritual appetite to be directed toward God and satisfied by God. This is a far cry from human ambition that seeks to advance itself in power and prestige. Quite the opposite in fact.

Let's use another graphic to represent this intrinsic connection, this linkage between each principle—and how this transformational cycle never ends (see next page).

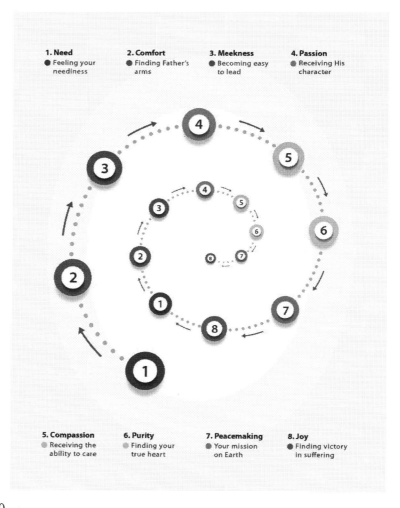

1. Need
● Feeling your neediness

2. Comfort
● Finding Father's arms

3. Meekness
● Becoming easy to lead

4. Passion
● Receiving His character

5. Compassion
● Receiving the ability to care

6. Purity
● Finding your true heart

7. Peacemaking
● Your mission on Earth

8. Joy
● Finding victory in suffering

As we saw in chapter four, we progress up the "mountain" via steps one through four, then down the back side, where the cycle begins again. Let's keep going.

As our souls find satisfaction in God's purposes for our lives, then we begin to feel what God feels—including love and mercy for those who are as needy as we are (blessing #5). It's not until we experience the reliability of God in our own lives that we can extend that grace to others in the form of mercy.

And we take another step.

Those who can hold and convey God's merciful heart to others are already on the road to purity of heart (blessing #6), which in turn prepares us for the redemptive role of peacemaker and friend of God (blessing #7). This level of integration into God's heart and God's ways then makes the idea of finding blessing in persecution more of a reality (blessing #8). God has earned our trust, so to speak, so we know how deeply safe we are in God's hands even when we are treated unjustly.

So the Eight Blessings all play into one another as their impact upon our lives accumulates. Our desires change. We begin to seriously value God's character more than our previous passions. It's the joy of receiving, not only forgiveness but Christ's gift of righteousness into our deep places that generates true satisfaction and contentment. Nothing else can touch this. It is true happiness. Enduring joy. This is the amazing life to which God invites us, all captured in utter simplicity in these eight short insights.

Leveraging Truth for Transformation

I trust that this brief book has invited you into a new measure of wonder and worship as you have reflected on God's Top Eight. Hopefully you have already been stretched and inspired towards personal change as a result. But that's the thing: we can learn things that don't necessarily change us. It's all in the application.

One simple yet powerful way to apply the Beatitudes in your life is to run a periodic check-in with yourself. *Where am I with these eight truths? Which one is front and center in my life right now?* Could you answer that question in this moment?

Are you being confronted by your spiritual need for God right now? Are you needing comfort? Are you being invited to yield to God's leadership and let go of your own control? Or is it passion...or compassion...or purity that is your current course in the school of the Spirit? Peacemaking is your ongoing mission. And the chance to experience joy in suffering will show up when hard times hit. But which one is on God's agenda for your blessing right this minute? Do you know?

Once you locate yourself on the circuit, dig into that truth proactively to cooperate with God's interior work. Just know that when you get to number eight (finding victory in suffering), it will feed you right back into the journey at number one again, feeling afresh your great need for God. Brilliant, huh!

Every day brings the invitation and opportunity to receive deep-hearted happiness—as you identify the gift you need most. The gifts are being offered freely...but until you recognize the need and receive the blessing, the gifts go unclaimed. Let's encourage each other to name what we need and live in the blessing day by day.

The Beatitudes are perhaps the most pithy, condensed summary of the path of light. Our map to freedom and celebration. So let's turn on God's GPS system to stay on the path of happiness and enjoy the life He's given us.

Glad to be on this journey with you!

ABOUT THE AUTHOR

 Jerry Daley is a veteran in church planting, having spearheaded six different church plants across North Carolina and South Carolina. After serving as a Captain in the US Air Force from 1964 to 1969, Jerry was called into ministry and studied at Fuller Seminary, Golden Gate Theological Seminary, and Columbia Seminary, completing the coursework for a D.Min. in 2013.

Jerry currently coaches, mentors, and trains pastoral leaders and teams. If you are interested in having Jerry work with you or your team, he may be contacted through the website www.jerrydaley.com.

Jerry and his wife Nan have three grown children, eight grandchildren, and one greatgrandchild. They reside in the mountains of North Carolina. His interests include physical fitness, reading, and endurance sports.

ABOUT THE SERIES

The *Follow Series* reflects a passion to uncover what it means to be a follower of Jesus in all aspects of life and ministry. As you know, "Follow me!" was and is Jesus' timeless call to men and women (Matthew 4:19). And so we seek to follow Him into thinking and acting and loving like Jesus. If you liked this book, be sure to pick up the others in the series, described below.

Book One: Following Jesus Into the Power

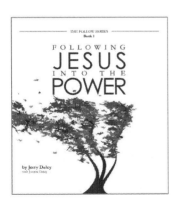

Have you ever found yourself wondering... where did all that power go?

The power to heal, physically and emotionally. The power to have the right words to say at the right time. The power to see people who are open and hungry—just like Jesus did—and lead them to the Source of Life. Is it possible for normal people to live that way too? Or was it just Jesus who got to do that stuff?

Your answer to that question changes everything! Join church-planter and leadership coach Jerry Daley on a real-world exploration to discover who the Holy Spirit wants to be in your life today. There is no reason to drift through your world powerless when Jesus' last words on earth were, "But you shall receive power when the Holy Spirit has come upon you" (Acts 1:8). It's time to power up!

Book Two: Following Jesus Out of the Brokenness

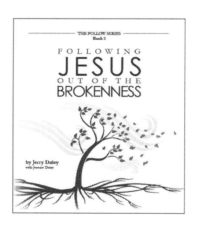

We yearn for meaning in a world marked by pain. How does the gospel lead us out of such brokenness?

Paul writes the book of Romans to describe how the gospel transforms, not just our eternal destiny, but our earthly future together. Personal suffering, relational rifts, behavioral addictions, church divisions, and even community fragmentation—all these are healed and restored by the gospel. This is Paul's promise to us. Dare we believe it?

Join Jerry Daley on a modern-day application of the heart of Romans to the urgent needs of local and global brokenness. Disappointment and disillusionment with the church will give way to fresh hope as we learn to not just *believe* the gospel, but *live* the gospel! Let's follow Jesus into His restoration project.

The *Follow Series* books are available on Amazon.com as well as Jerry's seminal work on discipleship, *Doing Life With*.

Made in the USA
Columbia, SC
04 August 2020

14344656R00052